POETRY THROUGH THE STORMS OF LOVE

BY: JASMINE AUTREY
Copyright 2018 Jasmine Autrey

Part I of this book is dedicated to A.G.W.
I have loved you beyond love and back.

Contents

PART I

Sleep Doesn't Come...6

Beyond Reality...7

I'm Only Human...9

We Are One...11

Without You..13

God Sent Magic 15

How Shall I Stop Mine Heart from Crying..17

I Still Believe in Us 19

Love Is Worth It 21

Did You Not Know 24

I've Come to Speak Love 26

A Long Time Ago 28

How Beautiful the Moon...30

It Doesn't Feel Right 31

Day to Day..32

Closure...34

Brave Face..36

My Heart 38

What I Should Have Said 41

PART II

Flawed and Still Loved 44

The Apple of His Eye 46

Love Questions...48

Let Me Love You 50

Play My Pain Away 52

Lead Us into Forever...................................54

Deceptive Dream 56

Fear..57

It Was You 58

Legs..60

My Lamentation 61

Paradise of Ecstasy.....................................62

Popping Buttons 63

Simple Complexity 64

Take 'Hold 65

Vulnerability..66

Well Done 67

What We Dream...69

Uncanny Bastard 70

No Tomorrow...71

I'll Be Strong for You...................................73

Depression 74

The Greatness of God 75

Try Harder..**76**

Love Fearlessly **77**

My Family and Friends...............................**79**

Little Black Girl..**81**

Sleep On **83**

Love, Show Yourself **85**

A Prince...**86**

Angelic Silhouettes **87**

Gaze Into Your Eyes **88**

Growing Pains **89**

He Showed Me **91**

I Will Remember **93**

Love Through **95**

No Apologies **96**

Not Your Stereotype......................................**98**

Words **100**

Pure Beauty...**102**

Some Kind of Woman **104**

PART I

Sleep Doesn't Come

7/10/17

Sleep doesn't come easily to me lately.
My body, mind, and spirit misses the one
who caressed and fulfilled them daily.
Devoid of their other half, they roam
around aimlessly,
hoping, praying, and fiending for the one
that they crave...who once craved them so
feverishly. Sleep doesn't come easily to me
lately.

Beyond Reality
7/11/17

The leaves rustle and whisper, illuminating
the reality of the wind.
My spirit moans and my bisected soul
laments bearing witness to our, perhaps,
inevitable love that we battled endlessly to
win.
The wind is a verity, but our love is beyond
that absolute; it is beyond reality. It
transcends past the physical and out of
reach to the senses.
It kicks down the boundaries of the norm
and evolves into spirituality…two kindred
but different spirits intertwined and fused
as one,
forged by the hands of God, a Damascus
and immortal love. A love that will live
even after our bodies must die,

I devoted myself to thee and you to I.
Our love goes beyond meager reality; none-
the-less, I vow to love you in my present
and with the totality of all that is and will
be me...if you promise our love can
continue through the bounds of reality.

I'm Only Human
8/7/17

I'm only human, no more but sometimes less.

Sometimes a savage, animal instincts take over, and it feels like I just have to have it.

The blood pounds and pounds and yells and curses my name.

My flesh wants to subdue, but my spirit knows that, in it, there is no Heavenly gain.

I'm only human,

weak and constantly tempted,

carnal, a derivative of what Eve did. I hate it,

constantly at war with the Devil because he wants me to settle and continuously live in sin, but I just can't get with it.

I'm only human,

but God has called me to rise against the

sinful and lustful flesh. He wants me at my
best.
If I have the Father, the Son, and the Holy
Spirit, then
the devil and his minions, the naysayers,
the haters, the insolent and the ignorant -
tsk, forget it. I'm only human, but, with the
Holy Trinity, I'm always killing it!

We Are One
8/20/17

Like a river flows through the mountains
creating a valley of new life and beauty as
it slowly diminishes the rock and earth
around it,
my love and essence traverse through the
depths of you giving birth to joy and peace
while meticulously eroding away the
misplaced and caged-up anger.
There is a calm that we can evoke in each
other because we are truly and spiritually
one.
Every part of me, down to the molecular
level, recognizes the synchronicity of your
heartbeat and mine, as well as how every
cell that encompasses you has become
complete upon our encounter, recognizing
in me its counterpart - the lifelong, sought-

after epiphany that tells your heart, "I
belong to her and she to me."
There is a peace and comfort that nuzzles
and dwells in our love, which produces an
outward glow of warmth in which we both
bask -
a sustained heat of passion that makes
onlookers and outsiders jealous and
envious. It incites inside of them a fervor to
make cold the love that we have for one
another,
but an infinite and immortal fire of love
such as ours shall ne'er be dimmed nor put
out. No devil in hell nor on earth can
extinguish the flames our hearts have
kindled within us. Fore with the love of
God on our side, we are one, united and
undefeatable!

Without You
8/29/17

Without you there is a pain so deep that it's
unspeakable,
even when I sleep the tears creep into and
out of my dreams reminding me that the
hurt is inescapable, the evidence soaked
and stained upon my pillow.
If the stars are the teardrops of the galaxies,
then even the galaxies haven't weeped as
much as my soul has wept.
The lightyears to Andromeda couldn't reach
the depths of where my pain is kept.
Without you, half of me is void. White
noise is used to fill in the gaps, but I know
that what my spirit lacks is you. The white
noise isn't strong enough to drown out the
pain.
No alcohol nor drug is powerful enough to

course through my veins and erase your
presence. Heck, I wouldn't even risk it!
Being with you is like heaven right here on
earth,
and without you...without you, I can't even
find the words.

God Sent Magic
8/29/17

We have that God sent magic,

that touch my hem and feel my power, feel

my aura type of magic. We make them

jealous and make them hate us.

Our God flows through us, and it shows.

We are blessed beyond measure, and they

know it! They can't do anything to stop it,

so they loathe us!

Defeated from the beginning, but they still

try to intervene.

They rally with the devil and his forces and

try to use his evil to split our team.

(Chuckles) Devil, please!

We have that God sent magic! The

nonsense, we get past it.

The haters make us go faster as they are

fuel for us to reach our destiny. The

bull**** won't prevent us from creating our own opportunities.

Call it that God sent magic that makes us unstoppable.

Being an opponent isn't wise. In order to survive, being a loyal friend is more probable. When you have it, you have it. Gates open, and doors close. Friends leave and in come the foes.

I don't fret it nor sweat it. We have that God sent Magic.

How Shall I Stop Mine Heart from Crying
9/17/17

How shall I stop mine heart from crying if I must brave this world without you? How do I pretend to be complete when the rib from which I came is no longer - snatched from me like a chastened child? Each sunrise and each sunset I hunger and thirst for you, for thine love - for the way your eyes spoke to the pit of my heart - for the way thine embrace clung to my soul. And each night as the stars burn with an indefinite, incandescent glow, mine heart starves in your absence. Mine sorrow floats on the surface making it impossible to see through or past whilst anger lingers beneath, heartbroken...all broken...that you left.

As long as you are gone, this heart o' mine

shall never stop crying.

I Still Believe in Us
9/19/17

Hopelessness of a future with you has not yet crept into my spirit. I do not believe that it ever shall; I still believe in us. For I can still remember so vividly and still feel the tugging and pushing on my spirit from when I first recognized your presence. Your spirit persistently poked at mine until I understood the divine language being spoken. 'Twas a force and gravitation so steadfast and so sovereign - a tongue and translation that mine spiritual ears had never known before that moment. It simply urged me to get to know you, to understand you, but its undertones whispered and stirred words into my soul like purpose and destiny. In an unknowing and pure-intentioned state, I obliged, and oh how the joy that you have brought me has overflowed and poured from me as the sun's light floods the earth. No matter what darkness may try to creep into love or regardless of the flashes of that are temporarily dimmed to a lustre, I know that our bioluminescence can outshine it all; I still believe in us.

Love Is Worth It
10/8/17

There will be times when that wretched pain uninvitedly becomes the only scenery you know, blocking the horizon and the beauty of such miraculous landscapes.

There will be times when you will want to doubt the very existence of love; however, love resides in each of us, for God is our creator and the epitome of love.

Therefore, love will never cease to exist. It may get buried and pummeled by the complications and pains of life, but love is worth it - to dig and dig beyond your hands' recognition, to put in the work to keep the person whose existence breathes life into your weary body and dampened heart.

Love is worth it because it takes us with our imperfections, holds our hand as we wade through the muddy waters, and is the very catalyst that makes us stand with an upright head and strengthens us to help us face and defeat our foes. Love is undoubtedly worth it. It casts a light on the darkness, but sees you through it. It tells you the truths you may not want to hear but continues showering you with love, washing away any bitter aftertastes. It walks beside you when you are fatigued, giving you a shoulder on which to lean. It runs with you and gives you encouragement as it helps you make it to the top, and it jogs beside you warning you to keep a steady pace as you trot through this journey that we only get once.

When the enemy attacks, love is always on guard - ready to fight, ready to pray or ready to nurture. When you have come close to the end of your travels with all of your souvenirs, wisdom, and stories that

guarantee a smile, no greater comfort nor
fulfillment will you get than from love
being nuzzled beside you, giving you peace
of mind.

Love is always worth it.

Did You Not Know
10/10/17

Did you not know that as the blood pumps
through my heart, it whispers your name?
Did you not know that the Earth quakes
because the weight of the love that I have
for you is too much for it to bear, while
simultaneously and paradoxically being as
light as the clouds that envelope us and
non-burdensome as the surrounding air?
How could you not know that, with you, I
see nothing out of our grasp? Everything is
attainable and just awaiting our summon,
and without you meaning vanishes and part
of my existence shrivels to nothing. How
could you not know that what we have is
the quintessence of love?
Did you not know? Did you not know that
half the value of life is lost absent of your

existence in mine? I need you and want you as you are a part of my lifeline, or did you not know?

I've Come to Speak Love
10/10/17

We are meant to express and extend that
which is in all of us; created via love, we
are expected to make that DNA
multiplicitous.
Love should be rampant and abundant and
running amok amongst us, for love is
limitless and ageless and dare not to be
contained by principalities nor boundaries
nor the hatred entangled within the races.
Love hates it!
So I've come to speak love and to speak life
to the dead places, speak healing to what is
perceived to be sickened,
speak peace to what has chosen to be
wicked, speak truth to whom and to where
the lies of the devil have been spread.
God loves you with an agape fervor. He

even has numbered every hair on your
head.

I've come to speak love, love, LOVE into
your spirit and into your mind. Call it a
paradigm shift from the dark to the light, a
reawakening of your life with the
introduction of Christ, Lasik vision for your
spirit - no more blurry sight, you can now
see clearly.

Now, please hear me. I've just come...to
speak love.

A Long Time Ago
10/12/17

A long time ago doesn't exist.

Every time that we touched to the moment
of our first kiss, I can still feel as if the time
in-between was nonexistent.

Every minute was real and rare, and every
memory that we shared, I feel it. I can close
my eyes and reach out and touch it...touch
you and touch us. A long time ago means
nothing to our love.

Time doesn't separate, in my mind, the air
that we breathed together nor the
experiences that we impressed on one
another.

It only creates lines and stanzas of infinite
love letters and poems of feelings and new
beginnings that I will never forget.

When it comes to our love, no, a long time

ago does not exist.

How Beautiful the Moon
10/12/17

How beautiful the moon looks tonight,
well-endowed and plastered against a
perfect night's sky.
Every star showed up to grace me with
their own lullaby as they twinkled twinkled
throughout the night's eye.
What great sorrow this experience brought,
to witness such resplendence when my love
is in such a drought,
to bear the burden of the potentiality that
such sceneries may only be observed and
shared by a lone me...void of you...Oh! the
tragic, imperceptible eventuality.
How beautiful the moon looks tonight, but
'tis not even worth the mention sans the
love and light of my life.

It Doesn't Feel Right
10/22/17

Life doesn't feel right without you.

The little victories and great conquers are

devalued without you there to share and

partake in the win.

The disappointing moments turn into a

stormy day without your love and warmth

to outshine the gloom.

My walk and my sway and the way I would

sashay sometimes goes offbeat because my

lifeline and I are no longer in sync.

Yes, life goes on without you, but the

happiness isn't the same.

It just doesn't feel right.

Day to Day
10/28/17

It tickles my curiosity to imagine a
relationship where we love day by day,
never forgetting that the present is as
precious as the pounds of air that we inhale
at constant intervals, or just the mere fact
that we have the capability of inhalation to
feed oxygen to a needy heart.
It requires nutrients and maintenance and
upkeep, but it also requires love even more
so than the blood and plasma itself. For to
live without love voids the meaning and the
pleasures of life. A sporadic love is a
selfish beast, showing up to make its
presence known only to get something in
return, pretending that it is the world's most
valuable treasure solely to edify itself - a
temporary high.

How I dream of a day to day renewal of forgiveness and of love! Perhaps with it, the anger and trivial aggravations dissipate because love is ever patient and always kind.

It bears with grace the burdens and shortcomings and the small defeats of life, using love as an industrial, spiritual vehicle to carry it all.

A day to day love seeks to constantly uplift and mend the broken, because mud thrown in response to a harsh word only makes both dirty and sullied. However, when God's overflow is pitched, both are made as clean as newborn babes.

Let us remind each other of our Father's love and express it to all at every chance and opportunity that we create. For a day to day love can save a soul any day.

Closure
11/3/17

The portion of me that was intertwined in you, that knew you better than anything else, which wanted nothing more than you, departed from me soon thereafter your departure. I, at the very least, now have a sense of resolve between us. I know that dreams of you will continue to trickle throughout my mind and both haunt me and arise the sentiments of happiness and joy.

We shared and created many ecstatic and awe filled moments while trying to better know and understand love with the challenges that are entangled in it and the lessons that it has taught us.

Having a greater insight and more in-depth knowledge of love is a joyous feat.

Although the limb that was nourished and grew as a result of our love has been severed and has seemingly vowed never to return to me, the love that has blossomed for each other inside of us, that we nurtured and pruned and from which we learned may be sufficient in providing me solace in my incompleteness. No greater gift could I have given you than love, and I have loved you beyond love and back.

Brave Face
12/2/17

I have to put on my brave face as I tell
my family and few friends that, yeah, I'm
okay,
as I masquerade around, hiding and
praying that my heart doesn't continue to
break and reveal the stress and the weight
of all of these heart aches.
I must put on this brave face now so that
underneath it impresses into my muscle
memory these rehearsed smiles and the
practiced laughter and the little kee-kee's
in hopes that when the brave face falls,
the bravery remains indefinitely.
This....brave.....face isn't just for me. I
have to be strong! I'm the rock! I'm the
shield and the arsenal for my family! The
protection and the bullets!

I stand on the frontlines taking shots and taking blows.
Elbows swing, and I duck thinking who threw it?!
If they only knew that they almost cracked my brave face...but it's okay. I'm determined to win it like I'm the only one running this race!
One day...one day, hopefully soon, I will be okay, but until then I will wear my brave face.

My Heart
12/6/17

When my heart is transferred to pump life into an unknown, fortunate soul, I wonder if they will see you when they close their eyes.

Will my heart, brought back to life, still beat off beat from when you said goodbye?

Will all of the memories that we created that are stained on my heart bleed into them?

I don't see them ever being washed or scrubbed away for anyone's sake.

Believe me; I tried! I cried oceans and cried seas, tried to simply forget but that darn ghost just continued to chase me and haunted me in my dreams.

Psh! Stupid memories.

I wonder if their blood will erode the millions of times that your name was etched into my heart...from every time that you made my spirit smile, brought out my womanly wilds, and helped us to take leaps and bounds in our love.

Will my heart, carved out of me and placed into them, still quiver and shudder from the experiences of ecstasy that your love brought to me...that bite my lips, clench my fists, "My God! This man is bringing Heaven to me!?"

Will they feel all of the joy and love that is stored in my heart pulsating through their body?

I pray that they do.

My heart knows pain, but through you, it has been submerged through the depths of love, seen the black abyss, and discovered treasures and wonders that it never knew. My heart displays these most precious jewels proudly with its many different hues from honeycomb yellow to ocean blue.

My heart is your heart's reflection, and it won't be the same until it's back at home, back at home with you.

What I Should Have Said
12/12/17

As the seasons change, as the nights grow longer, as the leaves fade and pluck themselves from the trees, as the heat shifts to a numbing, chilly breeze each day I long for you and reflect on what I should have said...and regret what I did not say.

As sure as the tidal waves beat upon the sandy shore and as sure as my heart beats and spells out your name, I promise you that my love can revive your weakened heart;

that's what I should have said.

I should have said that together we are bonded as one atom, and apart nuclear reactions occur because our love was never meant to be separated. Forcing it to part ways is like trying to separate the

Father and the Son, the Son and the Holy
Spirit, the Holy Spirit and the Father.
They are one as are we, from the creation
of time until it ceases to exist.
I should have said that even if you do not
believe in me at the moment, I know that
you believe in us and in our potential and,
more importantly, in the God in us.
Believe that with God and each other, we
can get through any obstacle that the
Devil puts in our path! Believe that we
are not our mistakes! Fight for us!
Believe in us! How can you give up on
what God ordained, what He sanctioned
and called to be?! How can you give up
on your heart...your soul's reflection?
THAT is what I should have said.

PART II

Flawed and Still Loved

Bruises, cuts, blemishes, and scars tell a story and a journey that hides secrets from us all. A flaw can be the tiniest of indiscretions that can taint the most precious stone.

What may appear to be tainted to you can be held as the greatest to someone who sees your potential and knows that you are more than this so called flaw or minor bump in the road. Flawed and still loved, is the song my soul sings.

My heart makes the melody so that my soul doesn't have to sing a cappella, but, sometimes, alone is what my soul often remembered.

However, whether harmonizing or singing a solo,

my spirit and my mind know that although I may be flawed, I am still loved.

But this love despite my imperfections

and excrescencies sometimes confuses
and perplexes me. How can you love me?
I am not spot-free.
A past with so many blemishes is not
merely blotted away. Drug through the
dirt and covered in thorns,
yet you see past all of that and love me all
the more. Your pearl is what you deemed
me. Flawed and worth millions, more
precious than diamonds and rubies
Because, in its rawest form, it's already at
the highest value it's supposed to be.
Flawed and still loved,
I love you simply for loving me.

The Apple of His Eye

My God is smiling down on me,

saying, "Look at my child, so beautiful
and living Holy."

And because of that, I'm reaping my

harvest and receiving what God promised

me. You can receive it too; you just have

to make the sacrifice.

Sin, lies, and death or everlasting life?

We all have to pay our dues, but Jesus

paid the ultimate price! He blesses those

who seek Him and bask in His love,

showers us with miracles as we say, "Oh

omnipotent one." My God is smiling

down on me, and I know He is proud.

I just want to let the Lord use me and

help someone else turn their life around.

Let the Lord use you too. He is greater

than you think.

He stretches from sea to sea and has the

greatest power of telepathy. He knows how you feel. He knows where you've been.

He can take the people you doubted the most and transform them to win. My God is smiling down on me, and He is smiling down on you too.

Don't believe the lies that the world feed you; stand on God's everlasting truth.

Make your wishes on Him, because He is THE STAR.

He holds the keys to the most luxurious of cars.

I want to hear Him dangle His keys as I approach His throne, see the pride glide off His lips as He says, "My child, well done."

Love Questions

How can love be timid and shy,

afraid to manifest and afraid to shine? How
can love back into a corner and hide?

When love has been beaten and has been

misused, love is often afraid to continue for

fear of being abused. How can love stare

down true love and turn away?

Because it was once stared down and was put
to shame.

How can love sabotage and try to end the

very thing it longs for and dwelled within? It

finds excuses and purposely tries not to make

it work.

Thinking, what if love gives love a chance

and suddenly there's a spark? What does love

do when it encounters real love?

Brick by brick and tear after tear,

love built a fortress around itself and posted a

post-it saying, "Love, you cannot enter here!"

So, what does love do when it encounters real
love,

knowing that there is this barrier between
them, and it just won't budge? Love does
nothing because if it's true love, the love
about which God speaks,

then the patience, and the kindness, and the
very essence of true love will seep into love
and enter it deeply, releasing its spirits and
kissing it softly and opening up love ever so
gently.

And the love of God will flow through those
bodies, restoring their souls and renewing
their minds.

THAT is what happens when love encounters
true love, and it is truly divine.

Let Me Love You

Let me love you like the sun loves the moon.
My love goes deeper than oceans and is truer
than the sky's light blue. You need me, and I
need you too.

You need my love to cover you and keep you
safe and warm.

You can find shelter in my heart as you lay
on my bosom, and I wrap you in my arm. Let
me love you.

Let me love you like God loved His only
begotten son.

We can both make sacrifices to help our love
grow like a plant that is nourished by the sun.
We'll watch our love blossom better than the
most beautiful of flowers.

Orchids, roses, tulips, our love shall never be
devoured. Let me love you. Your eyes tell me
of your pain.

You've been searching for someone to love

you, but you don't want you love to be in
vain. I can love you the way you deserve and
cater to your soul.

Keep your hidden treasures, my lips are
sealed and gold.

I can kiss away the hurt and unravel your
heart's true desire, which is to love as you
have been loved and set our souls on fire. Let
me love you.

I promise you wont be disappointed,

because this love I have inside is truly God
anointed. Let me love you.

Play My Pain Away

Last night I tried to play my pain away.

I wish I had an orchestra to create

symphonies, because when it's just myself

and my guitar strings,

the chords I strum and the notes I pick don't

fully express the inward cry that I want so

badly to scream! The inward cry that I want

you to see…but it can only be seen

metaphorically.

None-the-less, I tried to play my pain away,
and it provided me with some relief.

I dosed off and, soon-thereafter, I was in my

REM sleep…feeling lovely. Morning arrives,

and I hear a beep.

WARNING ALERT: This relief is only
temporary!

I sit up and look over and see the pain

dumbfounded and staring at me like, "You

thought you could leave?"

Well, dang!

I guess tonight I'll try it again, try to play my pain away and get it to end!

Lead Us into Forever

I surrender my hand unto yours as you lead
us into what we pray will be forever. Perfect
love casts out all fear, so your heart you have
given me to treasure.

Therefore, I will until death do us part.

Our two souls and spirits intertwined until
they combine, and one is no longer
distinguishable from the other.

My pain is your pain, and our happiness lies
in the inner beings of eachother.

I will grow with you so long as you feed me
as I crave for your touches and kisses and that
your words and heart and thoughts never
leave me,

because as a man thinks then so is he.

For out of the abundance of the heart, his
mouth speaks. I will say yes. Yes to a never
ending love story, Yes to us giving Him the
glory.

Together, we can do it as you lead us into
forever.

Deceptive Dream

I yearned and searched for your presence, but it I did not find.

Imagined your kisses along my neck, But

'woke and you were not by my side. 'Twas

dreams and flights of fancy,

Your hands dancing, dancing, dancing all

over me. O what a deceptive dream,

How it teased and seduced me,

Fulfilled me it did not. Curséd that deceptive dream.

Fear

Fear - a crippling element that oft' blurs
reality and filters out joy within,
a slave confined to a mentality
That does not excel thee into greatness. I
want all that God has promised to me! I want
all that God has promised to us. Whether
we're separate or together,
We cannot allow fear to hinder us.

It Was You

From the moment my soul felt the presence
of your spirit, I knew it was you.

From the moment I saw the King inside of

the king inside of the husband inside of this

awe filled being,

I knew it was you...

The one for which my love waited so

patiently, yet so anxiously. The reason why

prior commitments were never so deep,

because there was always one strong tie that

was anchored from you to me. I knew it was

you... The way my tears formed at the

thought of not having you.

The way the sorrows came, and it rained
again

because I thought your heart didn't have

etched in it my name. I knew it was you...

when the heavens and the angels stood still

because it could feel the chill

that danced through my body when you

perused your fingers over my silk. When I

drifted into your eyes and past lovers were

erased,

and the future with you was crystal as day! I
knew it was you.

Legs

I had dreamt of those legs wrapped around
you.

Your hands bold, gliding down them as if to

sculpture a masterpiece on a clay wheel, but

'lone they were, an isolated thrill.

My Lamentation

This is more than an "I'm sorry."
It's my lamentation and plea for new mercies
that are as fresh as the dew that accumulates
each morning.
My love letters, my love songs
aren't complete without you. The keys play.
The strings are strummed, but the sound is
opaque without the beat of your drum.
My hips want to sway to your rhythm with
your song stuck on my mind, forgetting all
the others because you take your time
as we go note by note and line by line, the
sweetest moans to the slowest grinds. I don't
know yet how to right my wrong,
but I do want to hear more of this wondrous
new song.

Paradise of Ecstasy

Time lies dormant while heads lie on the
clouds.

We'll revel in blissful magic, oil soaked
limbs and loins wrapped in towels.

Unravel your worries and rest your locks on

me as dreams come true and blur the lines of

reality.

A finger you shan't lift as the queen tends to
the king in this paradise of ecstasy.

Popping Buttons

I'm popping buttons and busting seams,
trying to get you as close as possible to me.
Skin against skin and sleeves and jeans shed
onto the ground beneath our feet, I love me
some him, and he loves him some me!

Simple Complexity

Love is simple in its complexity, but it never
ceases to perplex me.

It never fails to leave me astounded, to leave
me questioning just how powerful this
simplicity can be - how potent it is.

I love Him because He first loved me, an
ongoing love that's hereditary. Loves looks at
me and blurs my flaws,

a pristine picture of perfection, payments
paid on the cross. Love is as complex as an
infant or an innocent child, sometimes easy
to please but often difficult to understand.

A simple love that puts the power of healing
and transformation in our hands, simple in
theory but complex in reality because
humankind has to choose between two sides
– wrong or right. Love is simple in its
complexity, and

I choose love.

Take 'Hold

Take 'hold, and take control of me.
Enrapture me tenderly
as though the sun's burning gases would
cease. Whisper your heart in my ear, for thine
perfect love casts out all fear. Thou
intertwined in me,
and mine affections surrendering to thee. Be
bold. Take 'hold and ne'er let go of me.

Vulnerability

Vulnerability is not being afraid of getting hurt a little but afraid of not experiencing, not basking in all of the joys that love and being in love have to offer. For perfect love casts out fear; likewise, that fear can hinder the other from walking in their truth...that he/she is in love with the other. Do not allow your past or the past of others to rain on your today or tomorrow, to rain on your love. Embrace me. Embrace us while loving as God loves - fearlessly.

Well Done

The end is inevitable, but with a soul so special, the end is always regrettable in some form or way. We regret that it was so soon and yearned for you to stay, just a little while longer.

If you could have held on just a little bit longer, been a little bit stronger! But you were already as strong as you needed to be, an iron fist that offered protection and dared anyone to endanger her genealogy, her family. Yet, still as gentle as the autumn breeze with the butterflies gliding and the bright star warming, humming birds singing, and the angels rejoicing.

Radiant with a glow of love ferocious like the unruly sea, tidal waves crashing and the thunder rolling as the lighting whips through the clouds over the beastly sea.

Peace be still. She is with God and both with

me. My Madea, my love,
a child of God whose Father will say, "Well
done." Well done thy good and faithful
servant. You may enter my kingdom. You've
deserved it.

What We Dream

What we dream can set us free,
soaring to the top like a bald eagle above the
open seas. Lack of worry and no care
remains, the pain has paid off, and the
phoenix has risen again. What we aspire to be
can save our souls, a non-ending dose of hope
when life strips you to the bones. Dream,
dream like you've never known sleep,
and reach beyond the unimaginable, the
unfathomable, the impossible.
Run and fight with fervor for what you
destine to be, putting aside the socialist
notions that handcuff limitations to our REM
being...and dream!
Because what we dream can set us free!

Uncanny Bastard

Love can be an uncanny bastard.

We dive in head first, blind-folded, fingers crossed and haphazardly.

If only we could see

the future set before us, the lies that would

hurt us, the promises you wouldn't keep! That

uncanny bastard - love.

Because my love remained what I said it would be!

My love was anchored to you while you were

adrift at sea. THAT UNCANNY BASTARD!

But my love also forgives and believes more

in the God in us than the hurt in me. A hurt

that will seep from me and soak into you,

because no longer were we a separate two but

rather a single soul. Love, may you help us

render anew this hopeful, tattered soul

No Tomorrow

There is no tomorrow if we do not fight for it today. There is no progress if we just turn the other way. Divided we fall, but together we can reach victory.

Black, brown, yellow, and white stand out, but those colors we ought not see. Exposing our children to hatred from what 'they' did and what 'they' said, distorting their vision so that we miss the bigger picture,

the image of them being scared!

But, look Massa! Look! We's can read now! Escaped the physical chains, we's freed now! Now we're owning our own businesses, more of us on the t.v. screen, owning our own houses (living the American dream),

going to the same universities as you, have the same jobs as you, and marrying your kids and grandkids....JUST LIKE YOU did our sistahs!

Well...not really because their union wasn't
always voluntary, but that's for a different
day, a different story!

They are events that happened in the past, but
it's hard to get past that!

However, at some point we must all stand
united, lend a helping hand to justice and not
let the past re-ignite us

and cause us to burn and destroy the path to
being great. There is no tomorrow if we do
not fight for it today.

I'll Be Strong for You

Like the sky envelopes and holds up the
moon, I'll be strong for you.

I'd cry all your tears and carry you mile for
mile, If not only to see you smile,

to not have to be burdened with the sins of

Eve. Put thine hand in mine, and I'll

strengthen thee. My blood, my admiration,

my secret friend,

oh how mine heart shreds going up against

thine broken spirit, shattered and tethered to

an sullen end. Make me your candlelight to

burn that lonesome rope.

I can be strong for you; just tell me you still
have hope!

Depression

Depression, you tormentuous and sick bastard!

Nursing on the joy of those merely trying to find happiness and love in a world that's sinking faster and faster into the pits of hell!

Hell! I hate depression!

I hate the DEvil, and how he keeps PRESSing and PRESSing ON the beautiful beings that God created until there's nothing left!

Unrecognizable, completely disguised as though the person you knew and loved...LOVE...never existed. But I get it!

Devil you can't steal my joy! You can't steal my family! You can still my friends!

And there's no way in Hell that you could win! Freaking depression

The Greatness of God

The greatness of God is in all of us.

Some may have to dig deeper to reach their

diamonds, like those embedded in the

Earth's crust; simply believe.

Tap into your inner greatness, and watch
what you achieve.

Try Harder

What is it that I see?
I see love hiding behind a layer of fear
seeping through a façade of confidence. I see
pain suppressed,
waiting to be expressed then embraced by the
person you know you can trust so you can
take down your fence
that has the "No Trespassing" sign and the
guard dogs and at the top of the fence the
little spiral of barbed wire.
But not at an attempt to keep everyone away,
the message I transcoded is simply, "Try
harder." Try harder because I'm not sure
what to do.
Try harder because I want love, but some of
these feelings I'm not sure how to sort
through. We can work.
This can work; just please, try harder.

Love Fearlessly

I will set aside my past

and stories of relationships that did not last

and love fearlessly,

in hope that you will do the same. Then we

can ride on the wings of the eagle and soar

with love as does the air that God breathes.

Undaunted love stares the enemy in the eyes

and demands him to leave. Love fearlessly.

When you bloom, I, too, will bloom,

and we will mature together and bring forth

seeds that will dwell in my womb. We must

stand hand in hand,

my flesh in the grasp of your man-li-ness and

vow to do beyond the best that we can. Love

fearlessly.

In doing so, we will break through boundaries

and cast out fears and forge a bond so strong

that will make our Heavenly Father pleased.

El sangre de Jesucristo will rise up from the
bottom of the wells within us and overflow to
transform the world and carry our union to
the depths of eternity,
all because we will love fearlessly.

My Family and Friends

My family and friends, my family and my
friends

are the tree of life that intertwines with its

vines and its leaves and the roots and soil that

nourishes me.

Bloodlines buried hundreds and thousands of

feet deep beneath the rings as the wind blows

and carries the tune from the leaves while

they sing.

Some fall and wither away or blow away or

just say it's too hard and choose not to stay.

temporary like items put on eBay,

sold to the highest bidder,

auctioned off their friendship so they could
leave when things got bitter. And when those
leaves turn from green to shades of oranges
and browns, it's those roots down there that
are holding me up from the ground.

If the leaves fall and the roots remain... If the

leaves fall and the roots remain,

is it a blessing or a curse or just another lesson

learned? Well, it's the circle of life. You have

joy, and you have pain.

You give, and you gain.

Sow love, and you'll always win... my family
and my friends.

Little Black Girl

Little black girl, little black girl which do you choose, a black doll or white Barbie?

Little black girl, little black girl which do you choose, silky straight or kinky curly?

Little black girl, little black girl which do you choose, a childhood homie or a corporate suit and tie?

Little black girl, little black girl, which do you choose,

to stay true to you or lose your identity by trying to get by

because you need to feed your kids, and you want your career to thrive.

But you have to work twice as hard, if not more, to get the same jobs Bethany and Jill received, even though your overall credentials are better and have framed the same degree.

My hair isn't going to do the job. My skin color isn't going to either!

If that's the case, then you should change

your signs to "Only Whites Hired." But that
would be 'against the law,' and that would be
'wrong.'

Well here's an idea. How about you actually
do what's right instead of lip-syncing the
Kum- Bay-Yah song!

Little black girls, little black girls I choose to
be me.

Someone has to stand for our rights, the right
to be me and the right to be you. Which do
you choose?

Sleep On

The storm is frantic, and the stakes are high.
This mountain is about to collapse right
before my eyes! Will you pray with me for a
minute and help me intercede?
You're too tired. Ahhh, I see.
The waters may devour me. Perhaps, I can't
make it to the shore. No, no, I get it. Just
sleep on. Missed calls, non-responsive texts,
I continue to replay the last events in my
mind trying to recall some kind of offense.
No results found.
Then how is it that you present to me this
underlying frown? A friend huh? Yea, a
friend indeed Sleep on. You appear
unfamiliar to me.
This pressure doesn't apply to you, so the
urgency of this nature is foreign to you. You
don't have a clue that I'm suffocating and
reaching to you as a lifeline! Flat line,

jagged line, flat line, jagged line,

my pulse sporadically fades from panic

and terror and not knowing if this will

persist forever. When will these tides

calm?

Will you take my hand? Don't worry. Sleep
on…

Love, Show Yourself

Unveil your face to me so that its rays may
warm my skin.

Tainted visions of the most panoramic picture
invade your mind time and time again. So he
covers his eyes and shies away from it that
can set him free:

a love that is true and genuine, the love that
my Father has given to me. My love is too
gentle to hurt you, too tender to cause a
bruise.

I pray that your apprehensions are lifted
along with your spirit and that 'to love
unregretfully will be the path that you choose.
Love, show yourself, and to fear, I deny you.

A Prince

My Father's eyes are your eyes. My Father's
heart you hold. The love that He has given, in
your heart it thrives.

You're a phenomenal man, a Godly man, a
man who holds our Father's hand.

Nothing to me is more pleasing than to see a
young man living as Christ expects of thee.

You're a prince, God's son – a man in a
chaotic world who decided to live Holy.

Angelic Silhouettes

Sweet whispering silhouettes floating in my
ear, note after note the whisper grew
stronger. Crescendo, decrescendo and back
to the whisper I remembered.
A faint simmer of the softest harmonizing,
chased by electrifying, eye bulging tones
that send a chill to every harmonic bone.
It captivates your soul and takes control,
and, symphonic moments later, the orchestra
is gone. A physical dismissal, although ever
present within,
voices of angels never disappear; a silent
and transparent transformation occurs so that
a new life can begin.

Gaze Into Your Eyes

To gaze into your eyes,

to be able to witness the fervent yet pacifying
storm,

to hear each raindrop fall methodically and

rhythmically is like being able to watch the

earth form.

To gaze into your eyes is like seeing a

masterpiece, raw and rare and yet perfect, a

heart's surrendering select because it can

never forget how it feels....

to gaze into your eyes.

Growing Pains

Eroded dreams and weathered visions, a
childhood love becomes a leaf in the wind.
Cracks and hairlines from years of stress
and perspire,
Just like that concrete, time knew we
couldn't be together. Morning fog to my
morning dew. Now I am the sunrise, and
you are the sunset.
Time zones apart and
those similarities no longer
connect. Growing pains!
They seem to have a
diverse and wide range.
From childhood loves to friends to dreams
you once fancied but now have estranged.
It perplexes even me how two can be thick
as thieves, form a Tee; I the vest, to your
sleeve. Then suddenly a bell rings, and the
good times created, the things we both

hated, the dreams and fears we confided…

Mean nothing.

These darn growing pains,

Shattering hopes then ricocheting off of a

piece of broken heart to pierce and burn into

the life of another innocent casualty.

It's a war!

To grow and to mature and to not grow
apart.

I pray that as we grow, we grow closer
together

And suffer the same growing pains that
bond us forever!

And as we live and learn, we teach each

other, so that your pains become my

pains to form a weathered letter and a

living testament,

saying you can endure the growing pains
and get the best of it!

He Showed Me

We never had any deep talks nor serious
conversations.

I believed that all he wanted to say, he said it

through his actions. How a man of God

should behave,

How the path of a righteous man is guided by

the Lord - He showed me. How a husband

treats his wife,

how a man provides for those whom God has

put in his life – He showed me. How a father

loves his sons,

how to give without recognition of what was

done – He showed me. How a father cares for

his daughters,

how a man upholds his family and presents

them to the Father – He showed me. I know

the acts of a real man, the love of a Godly

man,

the silence of a humble man because he has

showed me these values that I want in my
husband; my dad showed me.

I Will Remember

How could I forget such a beautiful soul?
Forgetting would be the epitome of
impossible, because it's impossible for me to
forget someone I admire. I will remember
how you inspired me and pushed me to reach
for what I was destined to be – Great.
I will remember the smiles given and the kind
words that you shared. A few years apart, but
I look up to you because you care.
You helped me to realize that my gifts cannot
be ostracized and thrown into captivity on a
deserted island. A star's brightness can only
be veiled for so long.
Eventually, the clouds pass away and the
illuminance from the star creates memories
that are too strong and too powerful to allow
time to crumble them as if they were never
born.
I will remember

because you breeze and glide by with an aura
of hope and the scent of strength,

which smells like David when he defeated

Goliath, when a single mother successfully

raises her tribe, or when you simply

overcome...

the opposition, the hater's critiques, the stares

and snickers that say you're less than what

you think, the blood that turned against you,

the friends that you loved who left you, and

all the traps they set to end you.

You overcame them.

You, my dear friend, I will always remember.

Love Through

If only we could love through the pain and
through the hate that the world serves us on a
silver platter and feeds us with a golden
spoon,

as if the torment that we will swallow from it
doesn't even matter. The pain being dished is
of no consequence to the waiter,

until karma comes along and invites himself
to dinner, and later is now as the hate peers at
you from the other side of the table.

What if we loved through the hate,

through all the manners of evil spoken
against you

and even when those manners of evil are
thrown against you... be it true or false?

The only way to change their heart is to love
them through it all. Love through the pain.
Shine love on their hate, their hard feelings,
and their disdain. Just love it all away.

No Apologies

I won't apologize for how I love.

I won't apologize for being passionate.

Forewarned that my love is strong, and you

said you could handle it. I won't apologize

for the fact that my love surpasses mediocrity.

I'm expected to love my best, because the
best love was first given to me.

So when I give the love that pumps through
my soul, I expect some level of equality in
the love that you try to give to me, especially
if you consider yourself to be closer than
anyone else is to me.

But, no, I won't apologize for my love.

I won't apologize for being as nice as

Gandhi, or as strong as Martin Luther King

Jr., as courageous and violent as Malcolm-X,

or as soft spoken as Maya Angelou, the

poetry queen.

I won't apologize for loving as deeply as

Noah Calhoun in "The Notebook," Love is supposed to be strong.

Anyone who disagrees or loves any less is doing it wrong.

Sadly, there are more people loving incorrectly than I would want to imagine it to be. However, I will apologize for you not getting the love need, for you having to get their water- downed version of love diluted with selfishness and no minerals that say that everything isn't about me.

I presented and gave you the epitome of love, but you rejected it because you were accustomed to this sub-standard version of love, too weak and too fragile to handle the strength of my love.

So, no, I won't apologize,

Because the love that I feed to you is the love that nurtures me.

Not Your Stereotype

I will not be another black female statistic or,
rather, stereotype. You know the kind; She
blames and hates every brother because of the
few who didn't treat her right. She
flamboyantly talks with her hands and pops
her lips,
dramatically rolls her eyes as she dips her
hips.
She is very combative with her words and
often quick tempered. No, I will not stand in
the shadow of this figure.
I'm proud of the skin I'm in, but I refuse to
be put within a box or category that is
supposed to speak volumes about me but
doesn't say a thing.
My boldness doesn't need to be loud.
My beauty doesn't need to be exaggerated.
A cloud of unfamiliar has-to-be's will not
define the woman who completes me. I'm

black by any means necessary,

as black as Martin Luther King Jr., and as
black as I was born to be.

I will not walk in hand with a set of criterion

that people of society deem or say I should be.

I am not your stereotype; I am me.

Words

A thousand words couldn't begin to describe

this love I have or these emotions I try to

hide, nor could they tell the tale of how much

I care,

how much I need you, and how much I want
eternity to be what this relationship bares.

At the end of the day, these words are just

words, spoken letters and syllables that

amount to some phrases which are void if my

actions don't portray

or speak volumes for what these words

simply can't say. They're just words.

Words that linger aimlessly in the

atmosphere, weightless unless they have a

foundation that can speak to fear and worry

and doubt -

a foundation so strong that the words are
mute.

Actions that are immensely powerful that not

a single word needs to escape from the mouth, because after it's all said, they're just words.

When the volume is turned down, what stories will your actions tell? Will the pages be blank or will you have bestsellers that fill up the shelves?

A meaningless word gains leverage when one's doings are more than average, and the deeds are not requested; instead, they just happen.

Words, nothing more and what you hear is what you get, so, please, save your breath. All I need is the evidence.

Pure Beauty

You're beautiful - a word often misused.
What you call scars and see as warped, I see
them as beauty marks. You're beautiful.
That translates to mean that I see your loving
soul and kind spirit and all the great things
our Father has called you to be!
Beautiful is quietly bold and exuberant in
essence, unique in its nature and terrifying to
cross because of the weight of it's presence.
Beautiful is intriguing yet intrigued by others,
ferociously loves, and unselfishly gives to
another. Beautiful laughs with life then leads
at light's speed.
You're beautiful inside and out, and your past
doesn't count.
All the negative encounters that formed
wounds on your heart and those wounds that
rose to the surface,
still beauty marks!

Nothing, nope, nothing, can negate or void
that fact that YOU'RE BEAUTIFUL!

Some Kind of Woman

It takes an extraordinary woman to love a
child extraordinarily. It takes a strong woman
to pour out her love to help blossom someone
else's seed. Very laudable and very virtuous
indeed!
A Godly woman whose shadow overcast me
allowing me to fill out the image that God
purposed me to be.
You're a wonderful woman, and I
cherish the ingredients you contributed
to aid in creating such a magnificent
recipe.
I know I am magnificent, because the
apple doesn't fall far from the tree.
Your deeply grounded roots will forever be
my anchor as my branches sprout leaves
and bear fruit from the years of hard work
and nurturing.
At the point of maturity they will fall,

remembering the droplets of wisdom that trickled down on them from mother but, more importantly, from someone phenomenal!

How fortunate I am to receive your love endlessly, a gift that gives and never returns empty. Thank you for being a mothering woman to assist in guiding me through the many stages that I will meet!

You'll always be one of my greatest fortunes; you are, undoubtedly, some kind of woman!

www.ingramcontent.com/pod-product-compliance
Lightning Source LLC
Chambersburg PA
CBHW062004040426
42447CB00010B/1911